PTSD!

"Endurance and Escape,
Writings of self-Consciousness"

By

BLUE SEVEN-SEVEN

¡Rompe las cadenas de la oscuridad!

Copyright © 2024 Blue Seven-Seven.

All rights reserved. No part of this book may be reproduced, stored, or transmitted by any means—whether auditory, graphic, mechanical, or electronic—without written permission of both publisher and author, except in the case of brief excerpts used in critical articles and reviews. Unauthorized reproduction of any part of this work is illegal and is punishable by law.

ISBN: 978-1-63950-234-9 (sc)
ISBN: 978-1-63950-235-6 (hc)
ISBN: 978-1-63950-236-3 (e)

This publication contains the opinions and ideas of its author. It is intended to provide helpful and informative material on the subjects addressed in the publication. The author and publisher specifically disclaim all responsibility for any liability, loss, or risk, personal or otherwise, which is incurred as a consequence, directly or indirectly, of the use and application of any of the contents of this book.

Writers Apex

Gateway Towards Success

8063 MADISON AVE #1252
Indianapolis, IN 46227
+13176596889
www.writersapex.com

CONTENTS

Endurance 1

"Breathe" 6

"The Game" 7

"Thoughts I received" 9

"Forever" 11

"Illusion" 13

"Love, Pain and Pleasure" 14

"Fathers, For Real" 15

"Twin Towers" 17

"Do Right Man" 19

"Unattached" 21

"The World In, Which We Live" 23

"The Why of Love" 25

"Fix It" 27

"He Was a Friend" 29

"Hero" 31

"If It Is Meant to Be" 32

"Just Let It Be." 33

"Love Is" 34

"Man What a Lady" 35

"Our Love" 36

"Love Significance" 37

"Love's Journey" 39

"Questionable Friend" 40

"What You Think" 41

"Life" 42

"Come Back" 43

"I Need One More Day" 45

"We Sleep Alone" 46

"They Call it Love" 47

Escape 49

Synopsis 53

ENDURANCE

They train us to go in to battle and be the best that we can be, upon our entry in the military. After our training, we were prepared to serve and protect. Now that we are no longer in the midst of battle or waiting for deployment. We find ourselves as civilians with no clear direction. The military did not train us to be civilians. They did not train us on what to do once we were done with our task of serving and protecting. So we asked ourselves, Now what?

Pain is a part of life's journey. It is not a condition, it is not a choice. Pain will touch us and we will feel it. We can accept it or we can try to reject it. No matter how it feels, it is a profound and truthful condition. If we choose to accept it; endure it as if we are on a never ending journey. Laugh as if we were a five year old, long before we knew the pain. Have fun whenever we get the chance and dance whenever we want, even if everyone is watching.

We think back, not able to erase the image of death and the looming fear of the everlasting nightmares of days filled with destruction long gone from our view. Struggling to shut out the site of someone you have known reaching out. Reaching out and requesting our help to rescue them from their inevitable death. We walk around as if we are unattached from the real world. Living with the fear of an unforseen and an unwelcome panic attack. Yeah, the panic attacks seem to be the worse part of our journey. The thought of being around others when we are going through a panic attack is terrifying. We wonder what others are thinking; (A) Is he/she crazy? (B) Is he/she losing it! It is terrifying, so that is the reason we avoid being around others more and more as time passes on.

We find ourselves drifting in and out of the past, desperately attempting to make a connection between the past and present. We do not have a choice if we choose to have a productive life and enjoy the people we love. In addition we are able to let them love us.

Have you ever found yourself bending over backward in an attempt to get along with a friend, love one and/or family member? I am sure you have. At times we just want a sense of peace. In order to achieve that sense of peace, we compromise our person as we know ourselves. Soon after, we suffer the negative effects while driving away and/or late at night while laying bed. We get angry and beat ourselves mentally over and over again.

In addition to compromising who we are as our person. In my studies I was able to learn about "Transactional Relationships" from article I read, written by Dr. Lynette Jachowicz, after reading her article, I am able to understands how our PTSD symptoms manifest in the form of transactional relationships. We often forge transactional relationships instead of building true heart to heart relationships. We build transactional relationships unconsciously as we are attempting to protect our feelings. We later realize the pitfall of that type of relationship and we demand more than we are able to obtain. We realize that our relationships are nothing more than business contracts. At Some point we recognize that the person has a role to play, and we have a role to play. Therefore, we each demand pleasure and our friends, lovers, and family seek rewards as they see fit. The relationship only becomes a problem when we fail to meet each others needs. IE, You refuse to loan them money or spend time with them; You are not allowed to be around to the grandchildren unless you behave in a designed framework of their parents expectations. Their parents, your children!

We seem to keep memories of unpleasant things in life. We do our best to put the past with the present, but it just will not fit. We tell ourselves that it is okay over and over again. We find ourselves sinking deeper and into the darkness. We continue to sink and grow a little more unattached day by day, night by night and person by person. We often wonder if we can really truly connect with anyone ever again.

As we get older or suddenly realize that we have gotten old as we catch a glimpse of ourselves in a mirror. Those are the situation dynamics of the way we see events of our pass. We often see others as well as ourselves distorted. Therefore, we must not allow our thinking to paint a picture of doom and destruction. The reality is that during those traumatic times, in most of those situations we were under an extreme amount of stress. It caused us to experience an episodic blackout. We were operating in a survival mode, we were doing things, but our brains were not recording. Note: We will never remember our actions and/or what truly happened.

I struggled with demons for years and I still struggle from time to time. **I remember back a few years ago, my sister said me, "Brother when I look at you I can't see anything behind your eyes, it's like darkness."** Fortunately, a few years ago when I became overwhelmed with the pitfalls of the military, I started writing. I soon realized that I was able to ease my bad thoughts and find a sense of calm. The following writings of self-consciousness have allowed me the opportunity to endure the memories and escape the pitfalls of the past.

Some of us may go through life for year struggling with thoughts and feelings of being broken. We need to know it does not matter what others say about us and how they treat us, we are not broken. They may say things (knowingly or unknowingly) to make us feel unworthy when we do not adhere to their demands of us. They must understand that we need to avoid particular situations and people to remain functional. Even if the people and situations being avoided is a result of being around and interacting with them. We have to learn and be willing to walk away, be okay and be productive in life.

Please scan the list of writings of Self-Consciousness. I am 100 percent sure that you will find a few pieces that will touch you and have a positive effect in your life!

"Breathe"

I can not seem to get any unfiltered air.

The darkness is overwhelming and unfair.

My head is spending out of control.

I hear the platoon sergeant
yelling from my fox hole.

It is as if we have been here for years,
but it has only been days.

The cold air is sliding though like a haze.

The never ending wounds of
military life is a disease.

The rain is falling harder and harder,
it is so difficult to breathe.

"The Game"

I do not understand the ways
to be part of relationships.

Others have obtained the secret, but
I missed obtaining it somehow.

I feel as if I am not even in the game.

The relationship game is passing me by.

I am led to believe that I am
plagued to be the referee.

I know the rules, but I am not
allowed to play, only referee.

I can see the joy and feel the excitement
of others as they play the game.

I can feel the joy and excitement,
but I cannot get into the game.

I take off my uniform and put my whistle upon the shelf, but my referee image remains.

In the relationship game, I guess I am destined to play the part of the referee.

Others do not hesitate when asking for my help on how to play the game, but they never ask me to play.

My fellow referees see themselves as victims.

They do not understand their destiny.

The joy and laughter astound me and I want so desperately to be in the game.

Looking out across the field as the game is being played, I realize that I am a referee, and I am part of the game also.

"Thoughts I received"

Do not spend major time with minor people. If there are people in your life that continually disappoint you, break promises, stomp on your dreams, being too judgmental, have different values and do not have your back during difficult times, that is not a friend. To have a friend, is to be a friend. (That is a lesson you must learn and accept early in life if you want to be a part of someone). Sometimes in life as you grow, your friends will either grow with you or go. Surround yourself with people who reflect your values, goals, interests, and lifestyle. When I think of any of my successes, I am thankful to my family and friends that have enriched my life. Over the years my phone book has changed because I have changed for the better. At first you think you're going to be alone, but after a while new people show up in your life that make your life so much sweeter and easier to endure. Remember, "Birds of a feather flock together." If you are an eagle, do not hang around with chickens: Chickens can not fly and they try in every way to keep you down on the ground with them.

"Forever"

I am in this place, it is dark and I do not seem to have much room, but it is secure.

I am safe here, forever.

I am down on my knees, but one day I will walk just like them, I am sure.

Somehow, I know it is true because I simply can not crawl forever.

Where am I? Look at all those girls and boys!

I guess I will be fine, but I could not bring my toys!

Will I ever learn my ABC's, never.

Through the years I have made A's not D's, I've worked hard, and others think that I am clever.

Graduation day has come and gone,
a day I thought would never be.

Oh, to go back to that place
where I was secure.

I think about that place, and I
understand the meaning of forever.

"Illusion"

Life appears to be in the midst of a cloud.

The sights and sounds aren't
coming in very clear or loud.

We did not take time yesterday.
So we say, "Let us do it tomorrow."
But we never say, "Let us do it today."

Why not now? Would it bring sorrow
or is the price to high to pay?

World events at present make our outlook
on life a multitude of confusion.

We believe this in each and every way,
but this could all be an illusion.

"Love, Pain and Pleasure"

Without the knowledge of pain,
it is impossible to appreciate
a moment of pleasure.

Without the knowledge of distance,
it is impossible to measure.

My dreams became reality the
moment I knew and loved you.

Before my knowledge of you,
I only knew pain.

With you, I began to experience pleasure.

I feel the joy of the sun on my face,
but I do not mind the rain.

The joy of love is important in any measure.

I feel as though I have been reborn.

You bring with you the joy of a rose
without the pain of its thorn.

"Fathers, For Real"

Fathers are men of misery,
when they are for real.

Fathers work hard at one job, sometimes
two in order to pay the bills.

Fathers fight harder than mothers to
be a part of their child's history.

Fathers work from sun up until
sun down in fields and mills.

Fathers struggle with the
joys of love and home.

Fathers are the blame for all
the hurt and pain.

Fathers never seem to be with their
children and they always roam.

Fathers are responsible for all
the days filled with rain.

Fathers never let their children have fun.

Fathers are given the task of making everyone hardy.

Fathers worry in the shadows while mothers soak up the sun.

Fathers always fund the feast, but they never get to the party.

Fathers are so misunderstood and never seem to be a part of their child's life.

Fathers are only called in times of despair.

Fathers cannot be friends with their children, they leave that for their wife.

Fathers are men with a pure heart, soul and zeal.

When they are really doing their task, for real.

"Twin Towers"

The economy was bouncing back.

The stocks and bonds were
on an upward track.

The GNP forecast had the best
results in quite some time.

Suddenly, everything changed.

In the early morning hours, someone
from the East committed a crime.

Our nation suffered a terrible blow,
and our lives were rearranged.

Someone from the East said, "I will
destroy those Twin Towers in the West."

They viewed the Twin Towers as a source
of evil against everyone in the East.

One man viewed the Twin Towers
and influenced the rest.

People in the East view him as a leader,
while those in the West view him as a beast.

Husbands, wives, sons, and daughters
paid the cost by getting hurt and killed.

Today, some of us continue to display
the American flag upon our chest.

Today, some of us continue to hope and
pray that our nation has healed.

Our nation along with others in world
will miss those Twin Towers in the West.

Have we really pulled together as one?

Are we as far apart as we have always been?

One fact still remains, there is someone in
the east looking at our way of life as a sin!

"Do Right Man"

She complains that her man never ever calls.

She looks out the window, paces
the floors and beats the walls.

In the relationship she gives all she can.

She constantly pleads with her
God for a Do Right Man

She meets you and you call her
each and every night.

But, she complains over and over
that guys never treat her right.

You listen to every word as close as you can.

You are able to digest her total pain
because you are a Do Right Man.

You realize that she has been hurt before.

You are aware that you did not
cause that pain. Does she know?

You forgive her for no shows and non-
returned calls. You are a Do Right Man.

She continuously explains to you how
she gave that last guy her all.

You soon realize that is indeed the case and
you should have read the writing on the wall.

So you stay and take all you can take.

No doubt, she wants you to pay
for that other guy's mistakes.

You continue the attempts to please
her in every way you can.

You realize after a period of time it's
extremely hard being a Do Right Man.

"Unattached"

He enjoyed being attached most of the time. It really felt and looked okay in the beginning. As usual, he found himself back at square one as time progressed. He knows he should have asked more detail questions in the beginning, but he felt [assumed —(ass-u-me)] He could trust his mate to tell him the important issues that would affect their lives. That was his problem! He knows he could not love her and felt guilt pretending. He did not want to keep playing with her affections and he should not keep going through that guilt situation. He has reached a point in his life where it was possible for him to love for the first time in his life. In order for him to love someone he has to trust them in every way. He knows most people can forgive and forget, but he does not work that way. His only solitude is writing, he could not clear his head any other way. He had to accept his Higher Power's purpose, for him being alone and unattached at that time and any other time in his life. He must trust his timing and remember, to everything there is a season, and a time to every purpose, including relationships. A good thing taken out of its appropriate season will be destroyed. If The Higher Power did not ordain a relationship for that time and season, it will lead to destruction.

"The World In, Which We Live"

How hard is it?

When will it get better?

The men that sit on their big
powerful horses astound me!

The slashing sound of their whips and
the loud commands quickly distracts my
mind as though the noise is thunder.

There is a great heritage that we
must somehow rise above.

It is the tremendous amount
of hate that has hindered our
Cities, States, and Countries.

Hate, has arisen because of differences
in Religion, skin color and gender.

The belief of equality and living as one people
is not possible in the world in, which we live.

That possibility is far from reach!

It is as though we are attempting to force our minds through neon fog in the air that hatred has made so thick that birds will not attempt to fly anymore.

The world in which we live has become susceptible to a disease that will not allow men to live up to their full potential.

It's sad but they never will, because of the difference in skin pigmentation, religious beliefs, and/or sexual orientation.

In order to build a better nation, we must rise above the built-in negative responses and prejudgments of others.

These prejudgments of others will continue to keep us in darkness, in the world in, which we live.

"The Why of Love"

Why is it so important to fight?

Why must we both be right?

Why is it so easy to look past love?

Why we can not see the pain and rise above?

Why is it so important for love to end as though it operates on an unscheduled stop?

Why must we be the one to
always come out on top?

Why is it so easy to fall apart?

Why is there so much damage to the heart?

Why can't we deal with the unspoken pain?

Why are the loneliest days filled with rain?

Why can't we show the love
that we truly feel?

Why can't we accept love in our lives and agree that it is real?

Why do we worry about love ending, before it even begins?

Why do we say, "I want to love you, but it depends?"

Why isn't it easy for us to see?

Just let love be!

"Fix It"

You can struggle with the
question of life with a smile.

Go deep into your past and remember
things you saw as a child.

The hustle and bustle of things
never made you quit.

You wish things were better in your
life and you want to fix it.

Your world seems unfair and
unjust in the dark of night.

You're frantic, nervous, and in
mist of a terrible fright.

You can struggle with things of which you
haven't control or you can simply smile.

You tell yourself, "I must fix it."

You fail to see the growth in letting
yourself struggle for a while.

Give yourself a chance to rest in order
to return with a sharper wit.

You come to me and complain of
the world and all its troubles.

I remind you now as I have before.
These issues are the same as those
of the Flintstones and Rubble.

"He Was a Friend"

We met on a well-traveled road.

He said, "Hello", I also bid my ado.

Seemed O.K., it was the acceptable mode.

He looked not like me, nor perhaps you.

Later, I needed help in my despair.

It seemed impossible, but I was able to cope.

He appeared and my despair
disappeared in thin air.

He gave me much more than hope.

"You owe me nothing," he said with a smile.

I thought to myself, I helped
someone in the past.

My destiny seems closer
now, not even a mile.

I have gone to so many places and oh so fast!

He and I grew up together; it's really sad.

This was so long ago, I can't say when.

Have I forgotten all the good that I had?

I didn't recognize it at times, but
he's always been my friend.

After a long road of trouble,
it was clear to see.

The friend I so desperately needed
turned out to be me.

"Hero"

How far should he look up to
ask someone to save him?

How far should he look down to
ask someone to save him?

Who should he ask to save him?

Who should he tell to save him?

To be saved, a hero must look
up to the person inside.

To be saved, a hero must look
down into the person inside.

To live life completely, A hero
must look into his soul.

He must understand that his
reality comes from is inside.

He knows no matter what, he has to be bold.

So at the very end, he is able to
relax an take his last ride.

"If It Is Meant to Be"

To obtain the true significance of life,
let us free ourselves and love something
greater than the act of loving.

If it is meant to be.

If we do not allow our life to
bring about joy and happiness

it will no longer bring about life.

If it is meant to be

Without fear, let us surrender
our life to a higher power and be
at peace with the outcome.

If it is meant to be, it will be.

"Just Let It Be."

I am missing you and you are missing me.

All we have to do is let it be.

I notice sometimes when you are not around,

I wish I could hug the image of
you that I have in my head.

I can smell the sweetness of your soul
with the profoundness of a bloodhound.

Our friendship will continue to
grow even if we never wed.

I am missing you and you are missing me.

All we have to do is let it be.

I am missing you and you are missing me.

All we have to do is let it be.

Just let it be!

"Love Is"

Love is filled with fear.

Love is a pain that comes
in the dark of night.

Love can hurt someone near.

Love is filled with dreams dulling our sight.

We deny, we lie and we
might even kill for it.

It comes with confusion, pain and
despair, but we never quit.

When we are down, it lifts us up.

When we are up, it brings us down.

Love is good, love is bad.

Love is fun, love is sad.

Love is love, love is love.

Love is!

"Man What a Lady"

To be with her is compared to floating above ground.

When I think of her it makes me stop and turn around

I am at my lowest; almost under the gun.

I think of her for a second and life is fun.

I wonder if I will always feel this way.

Who knows?

For what will or will not be, who is to say?

That is the way it goes.

"Our Love"

Reaching for yesterday and
remembering the good things.

We played, we laughed, and
we exchanged rings.

We promised to love each
other forever and a day.

As long as our love is meant to
be, we will make a way.

The two of us will soon be three.

A boy or a girl, you can hardly wait to see.

For him or her and you,
I thank the stars above.

Keep shinning on our love.

"Love Significance"

To obtain the true significance of love we need to free ourselves to love something greater than loving. If we don't allow our love to bring about joy and happiness, it will no longer bring about love. We need to give our will to a higher power and be able to live at peace with the outcome.

When I think of love, I'm reminded of my son as a small boy. He held his little puppy to tight because he did not want to drop him and hurt him. But he did not realize that he was hurting him by holding so tight. His puppy bit him and he dropped him. He looked at me with tears in his eyes and asked, "Dad, why did he bite me?" He did not understand and at that time I did not have an appropriate response to his question.

Most people are scared of losing someone they love, and they hold on to tight, not realizing the pain that they are causing them. For that, they will be saddened, because they have damaged a special gift in the process. The special gift of love once damaged is often beyond repair.

"Love's Journey"

"If you ever know love, love will remain in you."

When you find someone, you truly love, you become a different person.

When you find someone, you truly love, your outlook on life changes.

When you find someone, you truly love, you become someone new.

When you find someone, you truly love, you become a better person.

When you find someone, you truly love, you become someone happy.

When you find someone, you truly love, you find a deep enter pace.

"Questionable Friend"

Are you really my friend?

You ask me to talk a certain way.

You beat me down every chance you get.

I feel as if my mind and soul needs to mend.

Is it possible for you and I
to see a better day?

It has been changing for the
worst every since we met.

You insist that I hold up the
standards of the good book.

As times goes on it really does not matter,
because I have realized you are a crook.

"What You Think"

You tell me how to wear my hair.

You tell me what type of shoes to buy.

You tell me to treat everyone fair.

You tell me to be an up standing guy.

You tell me how to treat my daughter and son.

You tell me that when it comes to blessings, I have none.

I do not see how or feel that our lives link.

After all is said and done, it does not matter what you think.

"Life"

Life is somewhat like watching
a movie on television.

You are really enjoying it and
in a relaxed mode.

All of sudden a commercial pop up.

Do you not find that annoying?

Well, I find that annoying also.

But I realize that in order to see the
entire movie and not miss a scene.

Just like life's journey, I must find interest
in the commercials and watch them also.

"Come Back"

I feel myself drifting farther
and farther away.

I reach out for the paddle trying
to hold on day by day.

I hear voices from a distance calling me.

The sounds are not coming in very clear.

Darkness is fast approaching,
and it is difficult to see.

The liquid is rushing over and
over against my ear.

The rescue boat appears to
be floating out of sight.

I am trying my best to see the morning sun.

I keep drifting and drifting
through out the night.

If this water was not so deep I would run.

Last night I remember being in my rack.

Last night seem to be so far away.

I hear my mother's words,
"Boy you gotta pray."

I hear her words while yelling at the ship,
"Come back, come back, come back."

"I Need One More Day"

When you love too much, walk away.

When you love too little, walk away.

When you hate too much, walk away.

When you hate too little, walk away.

When you hurt too much, walk away.

When you hurt too little, walk away.

When you see too much, walk away.

when you see too little, walk away.

When we are experiencing situations that we do not know what to do, walk away, just walk away to live one more day.

"We Sleep Alone"

We struggle with the real trauma as we sleep.

We lay in bed afraid of our dreams of despair.

We count through the night, one sheep, two sheep, three sheep.

We find ourselves resting only to awake gasping for air.

We worry about the nightmares effecting our lover's rest.

We often sleep in another room to be our best.

As we worry about our gasp and a possible moan.

Time and circumstance allow us to sleep alone.

"They Call it Love"

When we all are born in a
family, everyone is there.

They take turns holding us up in the air.

We are looked at and examined
for a family trait.

As we grow we come to realize
the family member hesitate.

They teach us things that
they want us to know.

They teach us things from
the Bible on the go.

They teach us to say
"Lord ley me down to sleep".

They teach us to say "I pray the
Lord my soul to keep".

They abuse us when we do not
contribute as they think we should.

They want us to give to them
our all or we are no good.

Their wants and needs are most important
and they do not put anything above.

They take all they can from
us and they call it love.

ESCAPE

I will make one clear undisputed point. In the world at some point in our history, every group of people have suffered and gone through hardship. As people we must reach out and compete to be the best people we can be and become aware of the pain of others. We must build a bridge that binds us all in order to live a productive life. Just think, what if we allow others as guests in our lives, let them enter and remain in our non-threading environment. By doing so, I am sure we can benefit from that behavior.

The world is a great place. Our country is filled with an opportunity to grow in many ways. The opportunity is there for us to be the best we can be for each other. Instead of working against a person's efforts to be the best that they can be. Many of us seem to complain about others not paying their fair share, while we make an effort not to pay anything toward the growth of the world. We appear to be self-serving in our efforts to control t he narrative of others. Example "We are the good guys and they are the bad guys". If a person is wealthy, in most situations they seem to be concerned about holding on to every dollar they can, while not having any concern for those in need.

When we find ourselves in a transactional relationship, we must find the wisdom and strength to walk away. We will be better for the people we truly love and for the people that truly love us. Please note: If we wonder whether or not someone truly cares about us. My guess is, they do not care about us. So we need to move on, because we are not responsible for their feelings. Fact is, we are responsible for our feelings only. We have to understand, life is tough and in order to remain healthy, we must be tough and live to be our best for the people we care about and love. We have to understand that when people lie to us, they do not love or care about us.

Generational trauma is a very important issue to consider. When interacting with our children, our grandchildren, our great grandchildren and so on down the line, we must make a concentrated effort to avoid passing our traumas down the line. Note: If we are unable to let go of our trauma in a healthy way, we stand the risk of negatively effecting our children, our grandchildren, our great grandchildren and on down the bloodline.

I am reminded of the importance of managing our trauma as I remember a story my friend shared with me. He said his grandfather asked him, "David, if you find yourself and your family down in a hole as the result of storm destroying your community, who would you help out first?" He told him, "I would help my wife out of the hole and then the kids." His grandfather told him that would be foolish. He asked him why. His grandfather said, "Because you would still be down in the hole. And who would take care of your wife and kids? You are still down in the hole, and they will not have the strength to pull you out. They will not be able to survive in life on their own. What you should do is have your wife and kids help you get out of the hole and then have the kids help you get your wife out and you and your wife can help each other get the kids out of the hole." Note: In order to keep the people we love safe, we must make sure we are safe.

To anyone struggling with ideas placed on them by others and feel threatened. Please take some time and apply a little introspection to come to grip with who you are as a person. Hopefully you will come to understand who you are , and be okay. Above all else, when you notice that you do not like someone, take time to evaluate why. I challenge everyone as a people, to make an attempt to reach out for the survival of human kind.

Believe us, we know giving up may seem easier than the struggling at times. Note: If we are struggling with life's situations, just hold on, reach out and remember; Suicide is not the answer, harming others is not the answer, or wasting away and letting yourself go, is not the answer.

P T S D is a real life situation, we are so guarded and we require a need for control over everything in our life. It is hard to move forward and enjoy life, family, friends and love ones, because of this life situation. Note: While in grad school, I read about an experiment on quantum mechanics call Schrodinger's cat. From what I remember, he put a cat in a box with a flask of poison and closed the box. After closing the box, he wondered if the cat had broken the flask of poison and died or if the cat had not broken the flask of poison and is still alive. The only way to know the reality of the situation, was to open the box. So, let us not avoid situations because we do not know how things will be for us. Let us move forward and find out what happens in each situation ("OPEN THE BOX").

SYNOPSIS

When reading "Endurance and Escape, Writings of Self-Consciousness" you will allow the author to take you on a journey describing the pitfalls and growing pains of our American active duty and military veterans. The author will also note the veterans' profound struggles while coping with day to day life surrounding family, friends and love ones.